TEA BREADS AND COFFEECAKES

TEA BREADS
AND
COFFEECAKES

ELIZABETH ALSTON

HarperCollins*Publishers*

FIRST EDITION

Designed by Cassandra J. Pappas

LIBRARY OF CONGRESS CATALOGING-IN-PUBLICATION DATA

Alston, Elizabeth.
    Tea breads and coffeecakes / Elizabeth Alston. — 1st ed.
      p.   cm.
    ISBN 0-06-016149-3
    1. Cake.   2. Bread.   I. Title.
TX771.A494   1991   90-55523
641.8′653—dc20

91   92   93   94   95   CG/RRD   10   9   8   7   6   5   4   3   2   1

CONTENTS

ACKNOWLEDGMENTS

With very special thanks to:

Ruth Cousineau, recipe
development associate

Sandra Robishaw and Miriam Rubin,
development and retesting

Paul E. Bolton and Dionisia Colon,
assistants

Marinella Cancio, word processing

INTRODUCTION

Come for coffee" has long been one of the nicest invitations to give or to receive. It evokes the aroma of freshly brewed coffee, and the anticipation of something delicious to eat while enjoying the company of one or several friends. "Come for tea" is an invitation that's quickly gaining popularity. It's easy to understand the appeal of both invitations. Neither occasion is hard to arrange and can be put together on the spur of the moment. There's no big deal involved as far as shopping, cooking, or cleanup go. Children can be included and can participate. Guests know the affair is likely to be short, a lovely few relaxing moments out of a busy life.

For the purposes of this book I've defined coffeecakes and tea breads as informal, homey baked goods that need no frosting or buttercream filling. Tea breads, for the most part, are baked in loaf pans. Made with baking powder and not too sweet, they are usually served plain but can be dressed up with ice cream or fruit for dessert. Today, in fact, tea breads often are used as dessert and certainly aren't limited to tea but turn up as a sweet accompaniment to morning coffee or even breakfast.

Coffeecakes include substantial plain ones suitable for breakfast, as well as slightly sweeter cakes, many streusel-topped, which are perfect as part of breakfast or on their own with coffee. There is also a whole chapter of delicious kuchens, traditional middle-European coffee treats, which consist of a soft cookie crust filled with fruit before baking.

Whether you are looking for a special coffeecake for a family breakfast, a cake that complements a glass of wine or sherry to serve to friends, a tea bread that's just right to take to a potluck supper or community gathering, or an easy refreshment for a committee meeting, you'll find plenty of easy-to-make ideas in this book.

HOW TO FOLLOW A RECIPE

Experienced bakers may skip this part.

Read a new recipe all the way through to get a sense of technique and timing. Note which of the three main techniques used is called for. None of them is difficult or requires special skill.

> *1. Mix-mix.* The dry ingredients (flour, spices, baking powder, baking soda) are mixed in one bowl, the wet ingredients (eggs, melted butter, sour cream, or buttermilk) in another. The wet ingredients are added to the dry and stirred gently until a well-blended batter is achieved. Wet and dry ingredients can be mixed separately ahead of time, but once the baking powder or baking soda is wet it starts to work and the batter should be put in the oven promptly.

2. Rubbing in. The dry ingredients are mixed in a bowl, then cold butter is cut in with a pastry blender (four semicircular strands of hard wire attached to a handle) or rubbed in with your fingers. The liquid ingredients are then added, and the mixture is stirred to make a well-blended batter or dough.

It takes just 3 or 4 seconds to "rub" fat into flour in a food processor, so if you have one, follow the food processor method.

3. Creaming. Room-temperature butter is beaten with the sugar to incorporate as much air as possible. The remaining ingredients are then added, the order depending on the recipe.

I've given food processor versions for many of the creaming-method recipes. The food processor incorporates little air, so the amount of batter is often considerably less and the baked cake may be smaller in size with a more compact texture. But for speed there is no comparison, and when tasting the food processor and mixer versions of a cake side by side, I have sometimes preferred the closer, denser texture produced by the food processor.

Make sure you have all the equipment and ingredients needed.

If butter at room temperature is called for, get it out of the refrigerator at once. Unwrap it and cut it into small pieces so it can soften while you continue preparations. (Butter can also be quickly softened in a microwave oven; for 8 tablespoons, allow 12 to 15 seconds on medium in a 650- to 700-watt oven.)

Unless the recipe involves up-front preparation such as peeling fruit, the next thing to do is to turn on the oven so it will be properly heated by the time the batter is ready to go in. Unless a recipe specifies otherwise, bake all cakes and breads in the approximate center of the oven. Before you turn on the oven, check that one rack is in the appropriate place.

Next, grease the pan if the recipe calls for it, even if the pan has a nonstick finish. Except for a very few recipes in which greasing with butter is specified, these recipes have all been tested with cooking spray—the plain oil kind, not the spray with flour added, although using that shouldn't pose any problem.

Instead of using a cooking spray, you may spread a thin film of butter, shortening, or vegetable oil over the inside of the pan with your fingers or with a piece of paper towel. Fat used for greasing a pan is in addition to any called for in the recipe.

With the oven heating and the pan ready, carefully measure the ingredients. Then make up the batter and get the cake into the oven. Since each oven has its own unique baking environment (which you learn to work with), the first time you bake a new recipe set the timer for 5 to 10 minutes less than the low end of the range given in each recipe. This first check should be just to make sure everything is going smoothly. The cake should be just about fully risen, or even fully risen, and the batter starting to dry out in the middle. Should a cake seem to be browning too quickly (and some ovens have a tendency to encourage fast browning), cover it loosely with a sheet of foil.

Baking times in a recipe are a guide as to how long a bread or cake will take to cook, but the most important factor is your own judgment. Use your sense of smell: When fully cooked, most cakes fill the kitchen with a good baked aroma. Use your eyes: If there's a puddle of wet batter in the center of the cake, more baking is needed. Use your sense of touch: Lightly press the cake in the center and, for comparison, at the edges. Your fingers will sink into uncooked batter; when the cake is cooked, it will feel springy.

If there is no obvious wet puddle in the center and if the cake is beginning to pull away from the sides of the pan, it is probably ready. Insert a wooden toothpick or skewer or a metal cake tester into the center of the cake and pull it out. The tester should come out "clean," that is, with no uncooked batter sticking to it. (With certain cakes, little bits of cake or fruit may cling to the pick, but their moistness is different from that of undercooked batter.)

If anything, it is better to slightly underbake a cake than to overbake it. A cake baked too long can be dry. Be assured that even very experienced bakers have doubts when it comes to deciding just when a cake is done.

Put the baked cake, still in the pan, on a wire cooling rack on the counter. Exactly how many minutes you leave it there is rarely important, but a minimum of 10 minutes is recommended to give the cake or bread time to firm up and for a slight steaming effect to help free the cake from the pan.

Now insert a thin knife between the cake and the pan and

go all around to make sure the cake is loose. (If the pan has a nonstick finish use a blunt tool, such as a wooden spreader, that won't scratch the surface.)

Unless the recipe specifies otherwise, turn the cake out onto the rack. A loaf cake will usually slide right out if you turn the pan on one side. Hold the cooling rack upside down on top of a round or square cake pan and turn the pan and rack over together.

If the cake is to be turned back over, gently hold it in your hands and turn it. Or place another rack lightly on top of the cake, hold on to both racks, and turn them over together (with the cake in the middle).

Some cakes are best eaten warm. Others benefit from being stored for one or two days at room temperature for the flavor to develop. Follow suggestions in individual recipes. Before storing, let the cake cool completely, then wrap it airtight. An easy way is to put the cooled cake back in the pan and overwrap it securely with foil. Or put the cake in a plastic bag (the zip-closure type works well) and squeeze out as much air as possible before you close the bag completely. A plastic refrigerator container is another good choice.

When freezing a cake, proper wrapping is essential to maintain flavor and quality. Plastic ''storage'' bags are not thick enough. Use bags labeled for freezer use.

To thaw breads and cakes, transfer them, still wrapped, to the refrigerator a few hours before you want to serve them. Or let them stand an hour or two at room temperature. To thaw a cake or bread quickly, unwrap it and let it stand about 5 minutes at room temperature. Slice it thin and

spread out the slices on a rack or countertop. They will be
ready to serve in about 10 minutes.

MEASURING INGREDIENTS

Accurate measuring is important to the success of baked
goods. Buy good-quality cup and spoon measures. They are
more accurate and last a lifetime.

For dry ingredients such as flours, grains, and sugars, use
metal or plastic measuring cups that come in nested sets of
1, 1/2, 1/3, and 1/4 cup. When a recipe calls for 3/4 cup of an
ingredient, use a 1/2-cup measure plus a 1/4 cup. Do not use a
1-cup measure and guess at the 3/4-cup mark.

To measure flour (also cocoa and confectioners' sugar),
stir it lightly in the bag or canister. Spoon it into the cup
measure until the cup is overflowing. Do not press the flour
down into the cup or tap the measure on the counter. Then
draw the back of a knife, or other straight edge, across the
top of the overflowing cup, sweeping off the excess. (Work
over the canister, bag, or a sheet of wax paper.)

To measure granulated white sugar and other flaky or
granular ingredients such as corn meal, oats, and oat bran,
scoop the ingredient from the bag or canister with the measuring cup, filling it to overflowing. Sweep off the excess
with the back of a knife.

To measure brown sugar, pack it firmly into the appropriate cup measure(s) with your fingertips until it is level with the top.

To measure teaspoons and tablespoons of dry ingredients such as baking powder, baking soda, salt, and spices, dip the measuring spoon into the ingredient, again filling to overflowing. Then sweep off the excess. Here's a tip from the *Woman's Day* test kitchen: Fasten a strip of Scotch tape tightly across the opening of a can of baking powder and use the edge of the tape to level off the baking powder.

Use a glass cup measure for liquid ingredients. With the measure on the countertop, pour in the liquid. Bend over and check the amount at eye level.

For semisolid ingredients such as yogurt or sour cream, use cup measures designed for either wet or dry ingredients.

NOTES ON INGREDIENTS

ALLSPICE. Not a mixture of spices but a spice in its own right; whole allspice is a hard, dark brown berry, slightly larger and rounder than a peppercorn.

BAKING POWDER AND BAKING SODA. These ingredients cannot be used interchangeably. When mixed with liquids, both cause bubbles (of carbon dioxide) to form in the batter, which raise or leaven or lighten the cake. Most modern baking powder is double-acting, which means it contains two leavens: one starts to work when mixed with liquid, the other is activated by heat.

Sifting has been eliminated from the recipes in this book, so when you add baking powder or baking soda to a recipe, make doubly sure there are no lumps. Should any be present, either put the powder in the palm of your hand and mash it smooth with the back of a spoon or sift it into the flour through a strainer (a tiny tea strainer works fine).

BROWN SUGAR. To remove the tiny lumps often found in brown sugar, either squish them between your fingers when adding them to dry ingredients or, if adding them to liquid, mash them against the side of the bowl and stir or whisk until they dissolve.

Brown sugar in a recipe may always be replaced with white sugar and molasses. Use 2 tablespoons molasses and 1/2 cup granulated white sugar for every half cup brown sugar called for. Add the molasses to the batter with the other liquid ingredients.

BUTTER. For baking I prefer the flavor of unsalted butter, but if you use lightly salted butter, reduce the amount of any salt called for. Margarine also works fine. Be sure to use regular stick or cube butter or margarine (or a butter-margarine blend). Do not use whipped, tub, or ''light'' butter, as the results are unpredictable.

CHERRIES. To pit cherries, you may use a large paper clip. Lift the inner curve of metal and bend it back so the clip is an elongated S. Bend the larger end slightly inward so it forms a teardrop shape. Hold the paper clip by the narrow end. Insert the wider end (the teardrop) through the stem hole and under the pit. Pull out the clip and it will bring both pit and stem with it. It takes no longer than 5 minutes to pit a pound of cherries.

FLOUR. Most of the recipes in this book call for all-purpose flour. You may use bleached or unbleached.

GRANULATED SUGAR. Means regular white cane or beet sugar (sucrose). Buy familiar brands or check the label. Do not use dextrose/sucrose blends now available in some areas. They aren't predictable enough for baking.

NUTS. To toast, spread out on a baking sheet or pan with sides. Bake at 350°F. (anywhere from 325°F. to 400°F. is fine) until the nuts smell toasted and are light brown in color, about 8 to 10 minutes. They will continue to brown slightly. If you wish, quickly tip them onto a plate to hasten cooling.

To save time, toast a double batch of nuts, then wrap and freeze the extra portion.

OIL. Can be olive or a good vegetable oil such as corn or canola. While making cakes with olive oil may seem radical here in the United States, it certainly isn't in Italy. Try it. Olive oil imparts a lovely flavor without being recognizable as such. Use ''pure'' or ''light'' olive oil for most cakes.

ORANGE OR LEMON PEEL. Use only the wafer-thin, bright-colored layer (sometimes called the zest) on the surface of the white pith. It contains the flavorful citrus oils. Scrub the orange or lemon and wipe dry. Use a grater specifically designed for peel; it has small V-shaped holes. You can find the same small holes in a typical four-sided grater or use the side that looks as if holes had been punched from the inside. Pull the fruit lightly but firmly across the grater in short, sharp strokes, removing just the colored part of the peel. Measure the grated peel, loosely packed, in a measuring spoon. Extra may be frozen.

SPICES. Store spices in a cool, dry place (but not in the refrigerator) away from the sun and the heat of your range. Good, full-flavored spices make all the difference in the quality of baked goods. When you open a new jar, write the month and year on the label. Replace ground spices after about a year or add a little extra to the recipe. Whole spices (cloves, cinnamon stick, nutmeg) do not lose their pungency but, except for nutmeg, are impractical to grind for baking. You can buy whole nutmegs and grate them when needed. Use the fine side of a grater or scrape the nutmeg with a paring knife.

VANILLA. Use pure vanilla extract.

ZANTE CURRANTS. Find these tiny dried grapes next to the raisins in your supermarket. They can be used interchangeably with raisins.

BREAKFAST BREADS

SPICY UPSIDE-DOWN SAUSAGE CORN BREAD

MAKES 6 TO 8 PORTIONS.

For a delicious breakfast serve sliced ripe mangoes or oranges followed by big wedges of this corn bread and sliced tomatoes. I like to include a few sun-dried tomatoes in the topping for little bursts of flavor. Be careful not to overbake the corn bread; it should be moist.

CORN BREAD

1	cup yellow corn meal
1	cup all-purpose flour
1	tablespoon granulated sugar
1	teaspoon baking powder
1	teaspoon salt
1/4	teaspoon dried oregano leaves, crumbled
1/4	teaspoon freshly ground pepper
1	cup milk
1/4	cup olive or vegetable oil
2	large eggs

TOPPING

1	package (12 ounces) hot breakfast sausage, thawed if frozen
1	ounce (1/4 cup) sun-dried tomatoes (optional)
1	large onion
4	ounces fresh mushrooms

CAST-IRON SKILLET, 9 INCHES ACROSS THE BOTTOM

If using plain (not oil-packed) sun-dried tomatoes, soak them in hot water for 10 minutes, then drain and pat dry with a paper towel. Heat the oven to 350°F.

To prepare the batter: Put corn meal, flour, sugar, baking powder, salt, oregano, and pepper into a large bowl. Stir to mix well. Pour in the milk and oil; break in the eggs. Beat with a wooden spoon, just until the batter is well blended.

To make the topping: Crumble the sausage into the skillet set over moderately high heat. Cook 4 to 5 minutes, until browned, stirring frequently and breaking up the sausage with a spoon.

While the sausage cooks, chop enough onion to make 1½ cups. Pour or spoon off and discard all but about 1 tablespoon of fat from the skillet. Add the onion to the skillet and cook 2 to 3 minutes, stirring frequently, until translucent. Wipe the mushrooms clean and slice them. Add to the skillet and cook about 1 minute, stirring often. Remove from the heat. Snip or slice the sun-dried tomatoes in strips, stir into the sausage mixture, and spread evenly in the skillet.

Spoon the corn meal batter over the sausage mixture. Place in the oven and bake until a wooden pick inserted in the center comes out clean and the corn bread feels springy, about 25 minutes. The corn bread should be pale.

Remove from the oven and let stand 5 minutes. Invert the skillet over a large serving plate. Spoon any topping left in the skillet over the bread. Cut into wedges and serve hot.

WHOLE-WHEAT DATE-AND-NUT BREAD

MAKES 12 PORTIONS.

A flavorful bread that is also very low in fat. In fact, you can make it practically fat free by using 2 egg whites instead of one whole egg and additional raisins instead of the walnuts.

8 *ounces pitted whole dates*
1½ *cups water*
1 *large egg*
1 *teaspoon vanilla extract*
1 *teaspoon baking powder*
1 *teaspoon baking soda*
¼ *teaspoon salt*
2 *cups whole-wheat flour*
½ *cup raisins*
½ *cup walnuts*

9 × 5 × 3-INCH OR 8½ × 4½ × 2¾-INCH LOAF PAN

Heat the oven to 350°F. Grease the pan.

Food processor method (hand and electric blender method follows): Put the dates in a food processor, squeezing each one to make sure there isn't a pit left in. Add 1 cup of water. Cover and process to a coarse purée. Add the egg, vanilla, baking powder, baking soda, salt, and remaining ½ cup

spread out the slices on a rack or countertop. They will be ready to serve in about 10 minutes.

MEASURING INGREDIENTS

Accurate measuring is important to the success of baked goods. Buy good-quality cup and spoon measures. They are more accurate and last a lifetime.

For dry ingredients such as flours, grains, and sugars, use metal or plastic measuring cups that come in nested sets of 1, 1/2, 1/3, and 1/4 cup. When a recipe calls for 3/4 cup of an ingredient, use a 1/2-cup measure plus a 1/4 cup. Do not use a 1-cup measure and guess at the 3/4-cup mark.

To measure flour (also cocoa and confectioners' sugar), stir it lightly in the bag or canister. Spoon it into the cup measure until the cup is overflowing. Do not press the flour down into the cup or tap the measure on the counter. Then draw the back of a knife, or other straight edge, across the top of the overflowing cup, sweeping off the excess. (Work over the canister, bag, or a sheet of wax paper.)

To measure granulated white sugar and other flaky or granular ingredients such as corn meal, oats, and oat bran, scoop the ingredient from the bag or canister with the measuring cup, filling it to overflowing. Sweep off the excess with the back of a knife.

To measure brown sugar, pack it firmly into the appropriate cup measure(s) with your fingertips until it is level with the top.

To measure teaspoons and tablespoons of dry ingredients such as baking powder, baking soda, salt, and spices, dip the measuring spoon into the ingredient, again filling to overflowing. Then sweep off the excess. Here's a tip from the *Woman's Day* test kitchen: Fasten a strip of Scotch tape tightly across the opening of a can of baking powder and use the edge of the tape to level off the baking powder.

Use a glass cup measure for liquid ingredients. With the measure on the countertop, pour in the liquid. Bend over and check the amount at eye level.

For semisolid ingredients such as yogurt or sour cream, use cup measures designed for either wet or dry ingredients.

NOTES ON INGREDIENTS

ALLSPICE. Not a mixture of spices but a spice in its own right; whole allspice is a hard, dark brown berry, slightly larger and rounder than a peppercorn.

BAKING POWDER AND BAKING SODA. These ingredients cannot be used interchangeably. When mixed with liquids, both cause bubbles (of carbon dioxide) to form in the batter, which raise or leaven or lighten the cake. Most modern baking powder is double-acting, which means it contains two leavens: one starts to work when mixed with liquid, the other is activated by heat.

Sifting has been eliminated from the recipes in this book, so when you add baking powder or baking soda to a recipe, make doubly sure there are no lumps. Should any be present, either put the powder in the palm of your hand and mash it smooth with the back of a spoon or sift it into the flour through a strainer (a tiny tea strainer works fine).

BROWN SUGAR. To remove the tiny lumps often found in brown sugar, either squish them between your fingers when adding them to dry ingredients or, if adding them to liquid, mash them against the side of the bowl and stir or whisk until they dissolve.

Brown sugar in a recipe may always be replaced with white sugar and molasses. Use 2 tablespoons molasses and 1/2 cup granulated white sugar for every half cup brown sugar called for. Add the molasses to the batter with the other liquid ingredients.

BUTTER. For baking I prefer the flavor of unsalted butter, but if you use lightly salted butter, reduce the amount of any salt called for. Margarine also works fine. Be sure to use regular stick or cube butter or margarine (or a butter-margarine blend). Do not use whipped, tub, or ''light'' butter, as the results are unpredictable.

CHERRIES. To pit cherries, you may use a large paper clip. Lift the inner curve of metal and bend it back so the clip is an elongated S. Bend the larger end slightly inward so it forms a teardrop shape. Hold the paper clip by the narrow end. Insert the wider end (the teardrop) through the stem hole and under the pit. Pull out the clip and it will bring both pit and stem with it. It takes no longer than 5 minutes to pit a pound of cherries.

FLOUR. Most of the recipes in this book call for all-purpose flour. You may use bleached or unbleached.

GRANULATED SUGAR. Means regular white cane or beet sugar (sucrose). Buy familiar brands or check the label. Do not use dextrose/sucrose blends now available in some areas. They aren't predictable enough for baking.

NUTS. To toast, spread out on a baking sheet or pan with sides. Bake at 350°F. (anywhere from 325°F. to 400°F. is fine) until the nuts smell toasted and are light brown in color, about 8 to 10 minutes. They will continue to brown slightly. If you wish, quickly tip them onto a plate to hasten cooling.

To save time, toast a double batch of nuts, then wrap and freeze the extra portion.

OIL. Can be olive or a good vegetable oil such as corn or canola. While making cakes with olive oil may seem radical here in the United States, it certainly isn't in Italy. Try it. Olive oil imparts a lovely flavor without being recognizable as such. Use ''pure'' or ''light'' olive oil for most cakes.

ORANGE OR LEMON PEEL. Use only the wafer-thin, bright-colored layer (sometimes called the zest) on the surface of the white pith. It contains the flavorful citrus oils. Scrub the orange or lemon and wipe dry. Use a grater specifically designed for peel; it has small V-shaped holes. You can find the same small holes in a typical four-sided grater or use the side that looks as if holes had been punched from the inside. Pull the fruit lightly but firmly across the grater in short, sharp strokes, removing just the colored part of the peel. Measure the grated peel, loosely packed, in a measuring spoon. Extra may be frozen.

SPICES. Store spices in a cool, dry place (but not in the refrigerator) away from the sun and the heat of your range. Good, full-flavored spices make all the difference in the quality of baked goods. When you open a new jar, write the month and year on the label. Replace ground spices after about a year or add a little extra to the recipe. Whole spices (cloves, cinnamon stick, nutmeg) do not lose their pungency but, except for nutmeg, are impractical to grind for baking. You can buy whole nutmegs and grate them when needed. Use the fine side of a grater or scrape the nutmeg with a paring knife.

VANILLA. Use pure vanilla extract.

ZANTE CURRANTS. Find these tiny dried grapes next to the raisins in your supermarket. They can be used interchangeably with raisins.

BREAKFAST BREADS

SPICY UPSIDE-DOWN SAUSAGE CORN BREAD

 ${F}$ or a delicious breakfast serve sliced ripe mangoes or oranges followed by big wedges of this corn bread and sliced tomatoes. I like to include a few sun-dried tomatoes in the topping for little bursts of flavor. Be careful not to overbake the corn bread; it should be moist.

CORN BREAD

1	cup yellow corn meal
1	cup all-purpose flour
1	tablespoon granulated sugar
1	teaspoon baking powder
1	teaspoon salt
1/4	teaspoon dried oregano leaves, crumbled
1/4	teaspoon freshly ground pepper
1	cup milk
1/4	cup olive or vegetable oil
2	large eggs

TOPPING

1	package (12 ounces) hot breakfast sausage, thawed if frozen
1	ounce (1/4 cup) sun-dried tomatoes (optional)
1	large onion
4	ounces fresh mushrooms

CAST-IRON SKILLET, 9 INCHES ACROSS THE BOTTOM

If using plain (not oil-packed) sun-dried tomatoes, soak them in hot water for 10 minutes, then drain and pat dry with a paper towel. Heat the oven to 350°F.

To prepare the batter: Put corn meal, flour, sugar, baking powder, salt, oregano, and pepper into a large bowl. Stir to mix well. Pour in the milk and oil; break in the eggs. Beat with a wooden spoon, just until the batter is well blended.

To make the topping: Crumble the sausage into the skillet set over moderately high heat. Cook 4 to 5 minutes, until browned, stirring frequently and breaking up the sausage with a spoon.

While the sausage cooks, chop enough onion to make 1½ cups. Pour or spoon off and discard all but about 1 tablespoon of fat from the skillet. Add the onion to the skillet and cook 2 to 3 minutes, stirring frequently, until translucent. Wipe the mushrooms clean and slice them. Add to the skillet and cook about 1 minute, stirring often. Remove from the heat. Snip or slice the sun-dried tomatoes in strips, stir into the sausage mixture, and spread evenly in the skillet.

Spoon the corn meal batter over the sausage mixture. Place in the oven and bake until a wooden pick inserted in the center comes out clean and the corn bread feels springy, about 25 minutes. The corn bread should be pale.

Remove from the oven and let stand 5 minutes. Invert the skillet over a large serving plate. Spoon any topping left in the skillet over the bread. Cut into wedges and serve hot.

WHOLE-WHEAT DATE-AND-NUT BREAD

MAKES **12** PORTIONS.

A flavorful bread that is also very low in fat. In fact, you can make it practically fat free by using 2 egg whites instead of one whole egg and additional raisins instead of the walnuts.

8	ounces pitted whole dates
1½	cups water
1	large egg
1	teaspoon vanilla extract
1	teaspoon baking powder
1	teaspoon baking soda
¼	teaspoon salt
2	cups whole-wheat flour
½	cup raisins
½	cup walnuts

9 × 5 × 3-INCH OR 8½ × 4½ × 2¾-INCH LOAF PAN

Heat the oven to 350°F. Grease the pan.

Food processor method (hand and electric blender method follows): Put the dates in a food processor, squeezing each one to make sure there isn't a pit left in. Add 1 cup of water. Cover and process to a coarse purée. Add the egg, vanilla, baking powder, baking soda, salt, and remaining ½ cup water. Process to blend thoroughly. Sprinkle the flour over the surface. Process just until blended. Sprinkle the raisins and walnuts over the top. Turn the processor on/off five or six times to mix in the nuts and raisins but not to chop them.

Spread the mixture in the prepared pan. Bake 40 to 45 minutes, or until a wooden pick inserted in the center comes out clean. Place the pan on a wire rack to cool for 10 to 20 minutes, then turn out the bread and turn it over. Let cool completely. Wrap airtight and store one day at room temperature before slicing.

By hand and electric blender: Chop the walnuts with a knife. Mix the flour, baking powder, baking soda, and salt in a large bowl. Add the walnuts and raisins and toss to mix. Purée the dates in 1 cup of water in the blender. Add remaining ½ cup water, the egg, and the vanilla, and blend well. Scrape into the flour mixture and stir until the flour is thoroughly moistened. Bake as directed above.

APPLESAUCE-OATMEAL
RAISIN CAKE

S oothing, nourishing, and stuffed with plump raisins. The finished cake is about 1 inch high.

1½   cups water
  1   cup old-fashioned oats
  1   cup dark raisins
 ½   teaspoon salt
  1   cup packed dark brown sugar
  1   cup unsweetened applesauce
 ¼   cup vegetable oil
1½   cups all-purpose flour
  1   teaspoon baking soda
  1   teaspoon ground cinnamon
 ½   teaspoon ground nutmeg
  2   large eggs

13 × 9-INCH BAKING PAN

Bring water to a boil in a medium-size saucepan over moderately high heat. Stir in the oats. When the liquid returns to a boil, stir in the raisins and salt. Reduce the heat and simmer 4 to 5 minutes, stirring occasionally, until the oats are soft and the water is absorbed.

Remove from the heat, stir in the sugar, applesauce, and oil. Cool to lukewarm.

Meanwhile, heat the oven to 350°F. and grease the pan. Put the flour, baking soda, cinnamon, and nutmeg into a large bowl. Stir to mix well.

Stir the eggs into the oat mixture. Add to the flour mixture, and stir just until all the flour is moistened. Spread in the prepared pan and bake 30 to 40 minutes, or until the cake starts to shrink from the sides of the pan and a wooden pick inserted in the center of the cake comes out clean.

Place the pan on a wire rack to cool. The cake is good served warm. Or cool completely, cover tightly, and store overnight at room temperature before serving or freezing.

WHOLE-WHEAT CARROT-APPLE HONEY CAKE

MAKES 18 PORTIONS.

Friends who appreciate the earthy flavor of whole-wheat flour will enjoy this. It isn't very sweet and is very good for breakfast, perhaps with a little cheese or honey butter.

2 cups whole-wheat flour
1 cup oat bran
2 teaspoons ground cinnamon
1 teaspoon baking soda
½ teaspoon salt
4 large eggs
¾ cup packed dark brown sugar
¾ cup vegetable or light olive oil
½ cup honey
1 pound carrots
1 pound Golden Delicious apples

13 × 9-INCH BAKING PAN

Heat the oven to 350°F. Grease the pan.

Put flour, oat bran, cinnamon, baking soda, and salt into a large bowl. Stir to mix well.

Put eggs, sugar, oil, and honey into another large bowl. Beat with a whisk until creamy.

Peel the carrots and shred in a food processor or on the

shred side of a four-sided grater. Wash apples and shred without peeling. Measure 3 cups shredded carrots and 2 cups apples. Stir into the oil mixture. (At this point you can cover and refrigerate the oil mixture overnight. Cover the flour mixture and leave at room temperature.)

Stir the apple mixture into the flour mixture until well blended. Spread the batter in the prepared pan. Bake until a wooden pick inserted in the center of the cake comes out clean, 45 to 55 minutes. Place the pan on a wire rack and let cool completely. Serve the cake freshly baked, or cover and refrigerate up to 3 days, or freeze up to 2 months.

VERY-LOW-FAT APPLESAUCE BROWN-SUGAR BREAD

MAKES **6** TO **8** PORTIONS IF THIS IS BREAKFAST,
10 TO **12** IF AN ACCOMPANIMENT
TO MORNING COFFEE.

A hearty slice of this moist, flavorful bread makes an excellent breakfast. Or carry a slice to work to enjoy with a cup of coffee. If you want to cut the fat to virtually nil, replace the nuts with raisins or Zante currants (add them at the end so they don't get chopped up) and the egg with two egg whites.

2	*cups all-purpose flour*
1/2	*cup packed dark brown sugar*
1	*teaspoon ground cinnamon*
1	*teaspoon baking powder*
1/2	*teaspoon baking soda*
1/4	*teaspoon salt*
1/2	*cup walnuts or pecans*
1 1/2	*cups unsweetened applesauce*
1	*large egg*

8 1/2 × 4 1/2 × 2 3/4-INCH LOAF PAN

Heat the oven to 350°F. Grease the pan.

Food processor method (hand method follows): Put flour, brown sugar, cinnamon, baking powder, baking soda, and salt into the bowl of a food processor. Process a few seconds to mix well. (Make sure the brown sugar is crushed.)

Add the nuts and process briefly to chop them fine. Add applesauce and egg. Process a few seconds to mix well.

Spread the batter in the prepared pan and bake until the bread is lightly browned and a wooden pick inserted in the center comes out almost clean, 45 to 50 minutes.

Place the pan on a wire rack to cool for about 20 minutes. Loosen the edges of the bread. Turn it out onto the rack and turn over. When completely cool, wrap airtight and store at room temperature several hours or overnight for flavor to develop.

By hand: Chop the nuts fine. Place in a large bowl and add the flour, cinnamon, baking powder, baking soda, and salt. Stir to mix well. Beat the egg and brown sugar in a medium-size bowl, mashing up any lumps of sugar. Beat in the applesauce until well blended. Add to the flour mixture and stir until well blended. Bake as directed above.

LAWSONS' PRUNE OAT-BRAN BREAD

MAKES 9 PORTIONS.

The wonderful intense oat flavor and aroma of this bread was inspired by muffins baked by Lawsons, a Washington, D.C., gourmet store. The high proportion of oat bran gives the bread a slightly sticky quality. This bread is good to eat warm for breakfast, about 30 minutes after it comes out of the oven; stored airtight at room temperature, it is even better the next day.

1   *cup pitted prunes*
2   *cups oat bran*
2   *cups all-purpose flour*
1/2   *cup granulated sugar*
3/4   *teaspoon baking soda*
1/4   *teaspoon salt*
1 1/4   *cups buttermilk or plain yogurt*
1/2   *cup light olive or vegetable oil*
1/4   *cup unsulfured molasses*
1   *large egg*

9-INCH SQUARE BAKING PAN

Heat the oven to 325°F. Grease the pan. Oil the blades of kitchen scissors or a knife and snip large prunes into about 12 pieces each, very small prunes into about 6 pieces.

Food processor method (hand method follows): Put the oat bran, flour, sugar, baking soda, and salt into a food processor. Process a few seconds to blend. Add the buttermilk, oil, molasses, and egg. Process 1 to 2 seconds to make a smooth batter. Scrape the sides of the bowl. Add cut-up prunes. Turn the machine on/off two or three times just to combine.

Scrape the batter into the prepared pan. Bake 50 to 60 minutes, until the bread starts to shrink from the edges, is firm to the touch, and a wooden pick inserted in the center comes out clean.

Place the pan on a wire rack to cool for 15 to 20 minutes. Turn the bread out onto the rack and turn over. Serve warm, or let cool completely, wrap airtight, and store overnight at room temperature before serving or freezing.

By hand: Put the dry ingredients into a large bowl. Stir to mix well. To cut cleanup, measure the buttermilk in a 1-quart measure. Add oil to the 1¾-cup mark and molasses to the 2-cup mark. Add the egg. Whisk with a fork or wire whisk to blend well.

Pour the buttermilk mixture into the flour mixture. Add the chopped prunes. Stir with a wooden spoon just until well blended. Scrape into the prepared pan. Bake as directed above.

BREAKFAST FRUIT-AND-NUT BREAD

MAKES **16** PORTIONS.
ALLOW **2** PIECES PER PERSON IF THIS *IS* BREAKFAST.

Unsalted farmer cheese (find it near cottage cheese or cream cheese in your market) gives this satisfying bread a complex flavor and damp texture. It also makes it more nutritious. You may use 1½ cups of Zante currants or raisins instead of the mixed fruits.

8	*tablespoons unsalted butter*
1¾	*cups all-purpose flour*
½	*cup granulated sugar*
2	*teaspoons baking powder*
½	*teaspoon baking soda*
¼	*teaspoon salt*
2	*large eggs*
	Two 7½-ounce packages unsalted farmer cheese
	One 6- to 8-ounce package mixed diced dried fruit (about 1½ cups)
1	*cup walnuts, pecans, or almonds, chopped*
¾	*cup milk*
1	*teaspoon vanilla extract*

9-INCH SPRINGFORM PAN

Heat the oven to 350°F. Grease the pan.

Melt the butter in a small saucepan. Pour into a large bowl; let cool.

Put flour, sugar, baking powder, baking soda, and salt into a medium-size bowl. Stir to mix well.

Whisk the eggs into the cooled butter. Add the farmer cheese, dried fruit, nuts, milk, and vanilla. Stir to mix well. The mixture will look crumbly and strange, not at all like a batter.

Sprinkle the flour mixture over the fruit mixture. Stir until well mixed. The mixture will still look lumpy and strange, but try not to worry.

Spread the mixture in the prepared pan. Bake 1 hour and 10 to 15 minutes, until the bread is very brown, springy to the touch, and starts to shrink from the sides. A wooden pick inserted in the center should come out moist, with perhaps little bits of fruit or cheese on it, but not totally wet liquid. If after 50 minutes of baking the bread seems very brown, cover it loosely with a sheet of foil.

Place the pan on a wire rack to cool for about 30 minutes. Loosen the edges of the bread and remove the pan sides. Serve the bread warm. Or cool completely, wrap airtight, and store 1 day at room temperature before serving or freezing.

MILO O'SULLIVAN'S CURRANT-NUTMEG SODA BREAD

MAKES **16** PORTIONS.

When my friend Milo was growing up in Ireland, this bread was baked over an open peat fire in a closed heavy iron "oven pot." Before the dough was put in, the pot was thoroughly heated and then sprinkled with flour. Hot peat was put on the lid of the pot while the bread baked. Milo remembers that his father loved bread and cakes baked over the open fire and thought there was no better way of cooking them. Even in our modern oven, this makes a wonderful dense, chewy bread that will satisfy everyone who craves "real" bread. It's as good with butter for breakfast as it is with cheese for a snack.

In hot, humid weather, start with 1¼ cups buttermilk and add more if needed. (If you forget and add too much, and the dough is unworkably sticky, scrape it without kneading onto the cooking sheet, sprinkle with sugar, and bake as directed.)

- *3   cups all-purpose flour*
- *¼   cup granulated sugar*
- *1   teaspoon baking soda*
- *¼   teaspoon salt*
- *¼   teaspoon ground nutmeg*
- *4   tablespoons unsalted butter, cut up*
- *1½   cups buttermilk, or 1 cup plain yogurt*

½ cup Zante currants or raisins, or ¼ cup of each
   Additional sugar for sprinkling

COOKIE SHEET

Check that one rack is in the bottom third of the oven and
heat the oven to 425°F.

Food processor method (hand method follows): Put flour,
sugar, baking soda, salt, and nutmeg into a food processor;
process a few seconds to blend.

Add butter and process a few seconds to blend. Add buttermilk and process 2 or 3 seconds until a dough forms.
Sprinkle with dried fruit. Turn the machine on/off two or
three times to distribute the fruit without chopping it.

Turn the dough out onto a lightly floured surface and
knead just enough to shape into a ball. Put the smooth side
up on an ungreased cookie sheet. Pat into a 7-inch round.
Sprinkle with about 2 teaspoons sugar. With a sharp knife,
cut a deep cross in the dough, cutting a little more than half-
way through.

Bake until the loaf is deep golden brown and sounds hol-
low when tapped, 35 to 40 minutes.

Transfer the loaf to a linen or cotton dish towel placed on
a wire cooling rack so that one half of the towel rests on the
counter. Cool 5 to 10 minutes, fold the other half of the
towel loosely over the loaf, and let cool completely.

Serve the bread on a board. Cut out one quarter at a time
and slice it.

By hand: Mix flour, sugar, baking soda, salt, and nutmeg
in a large bowl. Add butter and cut it in with a pastry

continued

blender and/or rub in with your fingers, until the mixture is in coarse crumbs. Stir in the currants.

Add the buttermilk and stir with a fork or wooden spoon until a stiff dough forms, adding a little more buttermilk or water if there is not enough liquid to moisten all the flour. Turn the dough out onto a lightly floured surface. Knead, shape, and bake as above.

COFFEECAKES

PECAN STREUSEL COFFEECAKE

MAKES 12 PORTIONS.

This is the perfect streusel coffeecake: a delicate base, lots of topping. You can bake it a day ahead. Or, the night before, mix the dry ingredients and make the topping; leave at room temperature. Combine the wet ingredients and refrigerate. In the morning, turn on the oven and take the wet ingredients out of the refrigerator. When the oven is hot, mix up the batter and you're ready to go.

10 tablespoons unsalted butter
2   cups all-purpose flour
1   teaspoon baking powder
1/2 teaspoon baking soda
1/4 teaspoon salt
3/4 cup granulated sugar
2   large eggs
1   teaspoon vanilla extract
1   cup reduced-fat or regular sour cream

STREUSEL TOPPING
1   cup pecans, chopped coarse
1/2 cup packed light brown sugar
1/2 cup all-purpose flour
3   tablespoons unsalted butter, at room temperature
2   teaspoons vanilla extract

Heat the oven to 325°F. Grease the pan.

Start the cake: Melt the butter in a medium-size saucepan (or in a bowl in a microwave oven). Remove from the heat and cool slightly.

Put the flour, baking powder, baking soda, and salt into a large bowl. Stir to mix well.

Add sugar, eggs, and vanilla to the butter; whisk to blend well. Stir in the sour cream.

Put all the topping ingredients into a small bowl. Work with your fingers or with a fork until the mixture is in coarse crumbs.

Add the sour-cream mixture to the flour mixture and stir just until well blended (the batter may be slightly lumpy). Spread the batter in the prepared pan. Sprinkle the topping over the surface.

Bake until a wooden pick inserted in the center of the cake comes out clean, 65 to 75 minutes. Place the pan on a wire rack to cool for 15 to 20 minutes. Loosen the edges of the cake with a knife and remove the sides of the pan. Let cool. If not serving the same day, wrap airtight and store overnight at room temperature, or freeze.

NUTMEG PLUM COBBLER CAKE

Wonderful served warm, fresh from the oven. Just as good the next day. Measure nutmeg carefully; too much can be overpowering. As the cake bakes, it bubbles up around the plums, hiding most of them.

1	*cup all-purpose flour*
1/2	*cup granulated sugar*
1	*teaspoon baking powder*
1/8	*teaspoon ground nutmeg*
2	*large eggs*
1/3	*cup milk*
3	*tablespoons light olive or vegetable oil*
1	*pound (about 5) ripe black plums (such as Black Beauty, Black Amber, or Friar)*

TOPPING
2   *tablespoons sugar mixed with 1/8 teaspoon ground nutmeg*

9-INCH ROUND CAKE PAN OR 9- TO 9½-INCH SPRINGFORM PAN

Heat the oven to 375°F. Grease the pan.

Put the flour, sugar, baking powder, and nutmeg into a large bowl. Stir to mix well.

Add the eggs, milk, and oil. Beat with a wooden spoon to make a smooth, thick, well-blended batter. Scrape into the prepared pan.

Halve and pit the plums. Halve again. Arrange them cut

side up on top of the batter. Sprinkle with the nutmeg-sugar topping. Bake until the cake is well browned and crisp on top and a wooden pick inserted in the center comes out clean, 40 to 45 minutes.

Place the pan on a wire rack to cool at least 10 minutes before serving. If keeping overnight, cool the cake completely, cover, and store at room temperature.

SIMPLE SOUR-CREAM SPICE CAKE

A satisfying cake that has a lovely flavor and texture. Sift a little confectioners' sugar over the top shortly before serving.

8   tablespoons unsalted butter, at room temperature
1   cup packed light brown sugar
2   large eggs
1   teaspoon baking powder
½   teaspoon baking soda
1   teaspoon ground cinnamon
½   teaspoon ground nutmeg
¼   teaspoon ground allspice
¼   teaspoon salt
2   cups all-purpose flour
1   cup reduced-fat or regular sour cream

9-INCH SQUARE BAKING PAN

Heat the oven to 350°F. Grease the pan.

In a large bowl, beat the butter and sugar with an electric mixer on high speed for 3 to 5 minutes, until pale and fluffy. Scrape down the sides of the bowl. Beat in the eggs one at a time. Scrape the bowl. Add the baking powder, baking soda, spices, and salt. Beat on low speed until well blended, continuing to scrape down the sides.

With mixer still running, add about ½ cup of the flour and, without waiting for it to be completely blended in, add about one-third of the sour cream. Add the remaining flour and sour cream in the same way. Mix only until blended.

Spread the batter evenly in the prepared pan. Bake until the cake is light gold in color and a wooden pick inserted in the center comes out clean, about 1 hour.

Place the pan on a wire rack to cool for 20 to 30 minutes. Loosen the edges of the cake with a knife and turn it out onto the rack. Turn the cake over and let it cool completely. Serve soon, or wrap airtight and let stand at room temperature overnight.

LOTS-OF-BLUEBERRIES COFFEECAKE

Best served warm, soon after baking, but still very good the next day. Use small berries if you can. Frozen berries work just fine; don't bother to thaw or rinse them.

4	tablespoons unsalted butter
3	cups (1 dry pint) blueberries
2	cups all-purpose flour
2½	teaspoons baking powder
½	teaspoon salt
¾	cup milk
⅔	cup granulated sugar
2	large eggs

TOPPING
2   tablespoons sugar mixed with ¼ teaspoon ground nutmeg

8- OR 9-INCH SQUARE GLASS BAKING DISH

Heat the oven to 350°F. Grease the dish. Melt the butter in a medium-size saucepan (or in a bowl in a microwave oven). Let cool. Wash and drain the blueberries; spread them out on paper towels to dry, removing any bits of leaf or stalk.

Put the flour, baking powder, and salt into a large bowl. Stir to mix well.

Add the milk, sugar, and eggs to the butter. Whisk to

blend well. Add to the flour mixture, stirring to blend well. Fold in the blueberries.

Spread the batter in the prepared dish. Sprinkle with the nutmeg-sugar topping. Bake until a wooden pick inserted in the center of the cake comes out clean, 50 to 60 minutes. Place the dish on a wire rack to cool at least 30 minutes before serving.

CINNAMON-RAISIN COFFEECAKE

MAKES **9** PORTIONS.

Good midmorning with coffee, or with tea in the afternoon.

8	tablespoons unsalted butter
1½	cups all-purpose flour
1	teaspoon baking soda
¼	teaspoon salt
⅔	cup granulated sugar
2	large eggs
1	cup plain yogurt
1	teaspoon vanilla extract
½	cup raisins

TOPPING

½	cup walnuts, chopped
⅓	cup packed light brown sugar
2	teaspoons ground cinnamon

9-INCH SQUARE BAKING PAN

Heat the oven to 350°F. Grease the pan. Melt the butter in a medium-size saucepan over low heat (or in a bowl in a microwave oven). Let cool slightly.

Put the flour, baking soda, and salt into a large bowl. Stir to mix well.

Add the sugar and eggs to the butter, whisking to blend well. Whisk in the yogurt and vanilla; stir in the raisins.

Mix the topping ingredients in a small bowl.

To make the cake batter, add the butter mixture to the flour mixture and stir just until well mixed. Spread about half the batter in the prepared pan and sprinkle with about half the topping. Cover with the remaining batter and topping.

Hold a table knife upright in the pan. Swirl through the batter two or three times to create a marbled effect.

Bake until a wooden pick inserted in the center of the cake comes out almost clean, 35 to 40 minutes. Place the pan on a wire rack to cool for 20 minutes. Loosen the edges of the cake with a knife. Invert the cake onto the rack, then hold a serving plate or another rack upside down on top of the cake and turn everything over together. Serve warm. Or cool completely, wrap airtight, and let stand overnight at room temperature before serving or freezing.

OATMEAL STREUSEL COFFEECAKE

MAKES 9 LARGE PORTIONS.

A tall cake, perfect for every day. Two kinds of oats may seem unnecessary, but the topping is not nearly so good if you use oat bran instead of big fat flakes of old-fashioned oats.

- 8 tablespoons unsalted butter
- 1 cup whole-wheat flour
- 1 cup all-purpose flour
- 1 cup oat bran
- 1/2 cup packed light brown sugar
- 1 tablespoon baking powder
- 2 teaspoons ground cinnamon
- 1/2 teaspoon baking soda
- 1/4 teaspoon salt
- 2 cups milk
- 2 large eggs
- 2 tablespoons unsulfured molasses, or an additional 1/4 cup brown sugar

OAT STREUSEL TOPPING
- 1/2 cup old-fashioned oats
- 1/2 cup all-purpose flour
- 1/4 cup packed light brown sugar
- 4 tablespoons unsalted butter, at room temperature
- 1/2 teaspoon ground cinnamon

9-INCH SQUARE BAKING PAN

Heat the oven to 350°F. Grease the pan. Melt the butter; let cool slightly.

Put the flours, oat bran, sugar, baking powder, cinnamon, baking soda, and salt into a large bowl. Stir to mix well.

Measure the milk in a 1-quart measure. Break in the eggs, add the melted butter and the molasses. Beat with a wire whisk to blend well.

Put all the topping ingredients into a small bowl and work with your fingers or a fork until the ingredients are mixed and the mixture is in coarse crumbs.

To make the cake batter, add the milk mixture to the flour mixture and stir just until well blended. Spread the batter in the prepared pan. Sprinkle the topping over the surface.

Bake until a wooden pick inserted in the center of the cake comes out clean, about 1 hour.

Place the pan on a wire rack to cool for at least 30 minutes before cutting the cake in squares and serving. If not serving until the next day, let the cake cool completely then wrap airtight and leave at room temperature, or freeze.

CHOCOLATE-MARBLED SOUR-CREAM CAKE WITH CINNAMON-ALMOND TOPPING

MAKES **10** to **12** PORTIONS.

Atreat for those who complain there is never enough topping.

6   *ounces semisweet chocolate (chips or squares)*
2   *cups all-purpose flour*
1   *teaspoon baking powder*
1/2 *teaspoon baking soda*
1/2 *teaspoon salt*
8   *tablespoons unsalted butter, at room temperature*
1   *cup plus 2 tablespoons granulated sugar*
2   *large eggs*
1   *teaspoon vanilla extract*
1   *cup reduced-fat or regular sour cream*
2/3 *cup toasted chopped almonds (see Note)*
1   *teaspoon ground cinnamon*

10 × 4-INCH TUBE PAN WITH REMOVABLE BOTTOM

Heat the oven to 350°F. Grease the pan. Melt the chocolate in a microwave oven or in a small, heavy saucepan over low heat, stirring often. Remove from the heat.

Put the flour, baking powder, baking soda, and salt into a bowl. Stir to mix well.

In a large bowl beat the butter and 1 cup sugar with an

electric mixer at high speed until pale and fluffy. Add the eggs one at a time, beating after each. Scrape the sides of the bowl. Beat in the vanilla.

Reduce the speed to low. Add about one-third of the flour mixture and, not waiting until it is completely mixed in, about one-third of the sour cream. Continue until all the flour and sour cream have been added, mixing only until blended.

Spread about half the batter in the prepared pan. Drop melted chocolate in spoonfuls over the batter and spread gently with a rubber spatula. Sprinkle with about half the nuts. Drop the remaining batter on top of the nuts and spread gently. Mix the remaining nuts with the cinnamon and 2 tablespoons granulated sugar. Sprinkle over the batter.

To create a marbled or swirled effect, hold a table knife upright in the batter, almost touching the bottom of the pan. Make zigzag "cuts" through the batter from side to side all the way around the pan.

Bake until a wooden pick inserted in the middle of the cake comes out clean, about 1 hour. Place the pan on a wire rack to cool for 20 minutes. Cut around the edge of the cake (and tube, too) with a knife to loosen. Remove the pan sides. Let the cake cool completely before removing from the pan bottom. Serve within a few hours or wrap airtight and keep at room temperature overnight, or freeze.

Note: Buy almonds that are already chopped and toasted. Or buy chopped blanched almonds (almonds with skins removed), spread them out on a cookie sheet, and bake 10 to 15 minutes at 350°F., until medium brown.

SOUR-CHERRY ALMOND CRUNCH CAKE

This recipe works best with pitted fresh sour cherries or with sour cherries packed in a can or jar. (Frozen cherries seem to exude too much liquid.) You need a 12- to 16-ounce jar or can for one cake. The 30-ounce jars that come from Yugoslavia yield enough cherries to make two cakes.

1   *can or jar (12 to 16 ounces) pitted sour cherries in light syrup or water; or 1¼ to 1½ cups pitted fresh sour cherries (see pages xvii–xviii)*
1   *cup all-purpose flour*
⅓   *cup granulated sugar*
½   *teaspoon baking powder*
¼   *teaspoon baking soda*
¼   *teaspoon salt*
4   *tablespoons unsalted butter, cut up*
½   *teaspoon almond extract*
½   *cup plain yogurt or buttermilk*

CRUNCH TOPPING
¾   *cup toasted chopped almonds*
⅓   *cup all-purpose flour*
⅓   *cup packed light brown sugar*
4   *tablespoons unsalted butter, cut up*

Heat the oven to 400°F. Drain canned cherries in a strainer or colander, then spread out on paper towels to absorb more liquid.

Put the flour, sugar, baking powder, baking soda, and salt into a large bowl. Stir to mix well. Add the butter and cut in with a pastry blender and/or rub in with your fingers, until the mixture is in coarse crumbs.

Stir almond extract into the yogurt. Add to the flour mixture and stir with a fork just until the mixture clumps together to form a soft dough.

Spread the dough in a thin layer in the ungreased pan. Scatter the cherries over evenly.

Put the topping ingredients into a small bowl and work with your fingers until well blended. The mixture will be lumpy. Sprinkle the topping over the cherries. Bake until the cake is golden brown and a wooden pick inserted in the center comes out clean, 30 to 35 minutes.

Place the pan on a wire rack to cool. Cut and serve the cake from the pan. Or loosen the edges with a knife before turning the cake gently out onto a plate. Then cover with a serving plate and gently turn both plates over together. If you store this cake overnight the almond flavor will develop more fully. But cover the cake loosely or the topping will lose some of its crunchiness.

SPICY PRUNE CAKE

Brown sugar and coffee add extra flavor to this moist, richly spiced cake.

1	cup pitted prunes
2	teaspoons instant coffee crystals
3/4	cup water
1	teaspoon vanilla extract
8	tablespoons unsalted butter, at room temperature
1 1/4	cups packed light or dark brown sugar
2	teaspoons baking powder
3/4	teaspoon baking soda
1	teaspoon ground cinnamon
1	teaspoon nutmeg
1/2	teaspoon ground allspice
1/2	teaspoon ground cloves
1/2	teaspoon salt
3	large eggs
2 1/4	cups all-purpose flour
1/3	cup walnuts, chopped fine

13 × 9 × 2-INCH BAKING PAN

Heat the oven to 350°F. Grease the pan. With oiled scissors or knife, snip or cut each prune into 10 to 12 pieces. Mix the coffee crystals with the water and the vanilla.

In a large bowl, beat the butter and sugar with an electric mixer on high speed for 2 to 3 minutes, until pale and fluffy.

Add baking powder, baking soda, spices, and salt. Beat until blended, scraping down the sides of the bowl. Break in the eggs, one at a time, beating after each. Scrape the sides.

With the mixer on low, add the flour about one-third at a time, alternating with the coffee mixture and beating just until blended. Mix in the prunes.

Spread the batter in the prepared pan. Sprinkle with the walnuts. Bake until a wooden pick inserted in the center comes out clean, about 45 minutes. (Be careful not to over-bake.) Place the pan on a wire rack to cool. Serve the cake warm. Or cool, cover tightly, and leave at room temperature overnight before slicing or freezing.

RHUBARB UPSIDE-DOWN CAKE

My mother pooh-poohed rhubarb, the first fresh "fruit" of spring, but next to apples it was my father's favorite fruit. He loved it stewed with red currant jelly for breakfast or dessert. Here the tart flavor of rhubarb makes a lovely contrast with the delicate, mildly sweet cake.

$1^{1/2}$ *tablespoons unsalted butter*
  About 12 ounces trimmed fresh rhubarb (do not use frozen rhubarb)
  2 *large eggs*
$1/4$ *cup granulated sugar*
$1/2$ *teaspoon vanilla extract*
  Few grains of salt
$1/4$ *teaspoon baking soda*
$1/4$ *cup packed light brown sugar*
$1/2$ *cup all-purpose flour*

9 × 1-INCH ROUND CAKE PAN

Heat the oven to 350°F. Cut the butter into small pieces and scatter it over the bottom of the ungreased cake pan; let soften while you continue preparations.

Trim the ends of the rhubarb and discard any leaves. (Rhubarb is often sold without leaves.) Wash and dry the stalks. Cut them into 1-inch lengths. You need $2^{1/2}$ to 3 cupfuls.

In a large bowl, beat the eggs, granulated sugar, vanilla, and salt with an electric mixer at high speed for about 5 minutes, until very thick and pale. Beat in the baking soda.

Meanwhile, spread the softened butter thickly over the bottom and lightly up the sides of the pan. Sprinkle the brown sugar evenly over the bottom. Arrange the rhubarb in concentric circles on top of the brown sugar.

Remove the bowl from the mixer. Sprinkle the flour over the surface of the egg mixture. Fold in gently but thoroughly with a rubber spatula.

Spread the batter evenly over the rhubarb. Bang the pan two or three times on the counter to remove any large air bubbles. Bake until a wooden pick inserted in the center comes out clean, 35 to 40 minutes. (Be careful not to overbake. There is very little fat in the cake and it can get dry if overbaked.)

Place the pan on a wire rack to cool for about 20 minutes. Loosen the edges of the cake with a knife and invert it onto a serving plate. Let cool at least 1 hour more before serving.

TEA BREADS

INTENSE CHOCOLATE TEA BREAD

This is good as is or with whipped cream and perhaps sliced fresh oranges for dessert. For the most intense flavor, use Dutch-process cocoa.

8   tablespoons unsalted butter, at room temperature
1¼   cups granulated sugar
1   teaspoon vanilla extract
2   large eggs
1   cup unsweetened cocoa powder
1   cup reduced-fat or regular sour cream
1   teaspoon baking powder
½   teaspoon baking soda
¼   teaspoon salt
1¾   cups all-purpose flour
       Confectioners' sugar

9 × 5 × 3-INCH LOAF PAN

Heat the oven to 350°F. Grease the pan.

In a large bowl, beat the butter, sugar, and vanilla with an electric mixer on high speed until pale and fluffy, 3 to 5 minutes. Scrape down the sides of the bowl. Beat in the eggs, one at a time, scraping the sides of the bowl after each.

Turn off the machine. Add cocoa, sour cream, baking powder, baking soda, and salt to the bowl. Mix in at low speed. When ingredients are well blended, scrape the sides of the bowl. Add the flour; mix only until blended.

Spread the batter in the prepared pan. Bake until a wooden pick inserted in the center comes out clean, about 1 hour and 10 to 15 minutes.

Place the pan on a wire rack to cool for 30 minutes. Loosen the edges of the bread with a knife and invert it onto the rack. Turn the bread over and let cool completely. Sift confectioners' sugar over the top before serving.

ORANGE SOUR-CREAM LOAF

The delicate flavor and texture make this a good cake to serve at any time. It is good plain with morning coffee or afternoon tea. For a glamorous dessert, present a slice on a small plate along with two or three slices of peeled navel orange; accompany with a bowl of whipped cream and a glass of an orange-flavor liqueur or a sweet dessert wine. Few people know or serve dessert wines, but I've always found that even the most skeptical guest quickly revels in the complex flavor a good dessert wine offers.

8	*tablespoons unsalted butter, at room temperature*
1	*cup granulated sugar*
2	*large eggs*
1	*tablespoon freshly grated orange peel*
2	*cups all-purpose flour*
1	*teaspoon baking powder*
1/2	*teaspoon baking soda*
1/2	*teaspoon salt*
1	*cup reduced-fat or regular sour cream*

9 × 5 × 3-INCH LOAF PAN

Heat the oven to 350°F. Grease the pan.

Beat the butter and sugar with an electric mixer on high speed for 5 to 7 minutes, until pale and fluffy. Scrape the sides of the bowl. Add the eggs one at a time, beating after each. Add the orange peel. Scrape the bowl.

Meanwhile, put the flour, baking powder, baking soda, and salt into a bowl. Stir to mix well.

With the machine on low, add about ½ cup of the flour mixture, and without waiting for it to mix in completely, add about one-third of the sour cream. Add the remaining flour mixture and sour cream in the same way, ending with flour. Mix only until well blended.

Spread the batter in the prepared pan. Bake until a wooden pick inserted in the center of the cake comes out clean, about 55 to 65 minutes.

Place the pan on a wire rack to cool for about 30 minutes. Loosen the edges of the cake with a knife, and turn it out onto the rack. Turn the cake over and let it cool completely. To store, wrap airtight and keep 1 day at room temperature or freeze.

DRIED PEAR, ANISE, AND WALNUT TEA BREAD

MAKES 12 PORTIONS.

The flavor of this bread gets better and better as it ages, so it is especially good to make when you're baking for a large tea party, committee meeting, or reception where you want to have most of the baking done well ahead of time. The slices are mottled brown and white, reminiscent, says one of my friends, of a beautiful calico cat.

1	cup water
8	ounces dried pears
3	tablespoons unsalted butter
3/4	cup granulated sugar
2 1/4	cups all-purpose flour
1	teaspoon baking soda
1/2	teaspoon salt
1	teaspoon anise seed
1	large egg
1	teaspoon vanilla extract
1	cup walnuts, almonds, or pecans, chopped coarse

8 1/2 × 4 1/2 × 2 3/4-INCH LOAF PAN

Bring the water to a boil while you cut the pears into 1/2-inch dice (about 1 1/2 cups) and put them into a large bowl. Pour the boiling water over the pears. Add butter and sugar and stir until the butter is melted and the sugar dissolved. Let cool until ready to use.

Heat the oven to 350°F. Grease the pan.

Put the flour, baking soda, and salt into another large bowl. Crush the anise seed in a mortar, or put the seeds on a board and crush them as fine as possible with the bottom of a glass cup measure.

Add the crushed anise to the flour and stir to mix well. Add the egg and vanilla to the pear mixture, and beat with a spoon until the egg is thoroughly broken up. Add the pear mixture to the flour mixture and stir just until combined. Stir in the nuts.

Spread the batter in the prepared pan. Bake until a wooden pick inserted in the center comes out clean, 55 to 60 minutes. Place the pan on a wire rack to cool for about 20 minutes. Turn the cake out onto the rack and turn over. Let cool completely. Wrap airtight and store at least one day before slicing.

MOLASSES GINGER CAKE

MAKES **8** PORTIONS.

Delicious as is for afternoon tea or with cheese for a light snack. Serve warm for dessert with just-melted vanilla or ginger ice cream. The flavor of the cake develops on keeping.

4	*tablespoons unsalted butter*
1	*cup unsulfured molasses*
1/2	*cup buttermilk or plain yogurt*
1/2	*cup packed dark brown sugar*
2	*large eggs*
1	*ounce crystallized ginger, chopped fine (2 tablespoons)*
2	*cups all-purpose flour*
1 1/2	*teaspoons ground ginger*
1	*teaspoon baking soda*

8-INCH SQUARE BAKING PAN

Heat the oven to 325°F. Grease the pan.

Melt the butter in a medium-size saucepan over low heat (or in a 1-quart or larger measure in a microwave oven).

Remove from the heat; stir in the molasses. Add the buttermilk, brown sugar, eggs, and crystallized ginger. Stir until thoroughly blended, mashing up any lumps of brown sugar.

Put the flour, ground ginger, and baking soda into a large bowl. Stir to mix well. Pour in the molasses mixture. Stir to blend well (a little tricky since you have a lot of wet ingredients and not that much dry). When well blended, spread in the prepared pan and bake until a wooden pick inserted in the center of the cake comes out clean, about 1 hour. Place the pan on a wire rack to cool at least 10 minutes. (The cake will sink a little toward the middle.) Serve the cake warm, or let it cool completely in the pan before storing airtight. Cut into squares.

QUINCE GINGER CAKE

This idea came from Jim Dodge, author of *The American Baker*. Buy about 1 pound ripe quinces. (When ripe, quinces are rock hard, of a yellow hue. Inedible raw, they have a wonderful flavor when cooked.) Peel and core the quinces and cut into rough 1/4-inch chunks—enough to make 2 cups. The fruit turns brown quickly; not to worry. Fold the fruit into the batter and bake as above.

GRETCHEN'S CRANBERRY-
APPLE CAKE

MAKES **12** TO **16** PORTIONS,
UP TO **28** THIN SLICES FOR A LARGE PARTY.

This recipe comes from my Seattle friend and restaurateur Gretchen Mathers. It makes a handsome cake that's a good keeper and is also quite low in fat. It's good alone or with a small scoop of vanilla ice cream. Sift a little confectioners' sugar over the top of the cake just before slicing.

2	cups all-purpose flour
1	teaspoon baking soda
1	teaspoon salt
1	teaspoon ground nutmeg
1	teaspoon ground cinnamon
2	medium-size Granny Smith apples
1¾	cups packed dark brown sugar
½	cup vegetable oil
2	large eggs
1	teaspoon vanilla extract
2	cups fresh or frozen cranberries
1	cup pecans or walnuts, chopped coarse

10- OR 12-CUP BUNDT PAN OR 10 × 4-INCH TUBE PAN

Heat the oven to 350°F. Grease the pan well.

Put the flour, baking soda, salt, nutmeg, and cinnamon into a bowl. Stir to mix well.

Quarter and core the apples (no need to peel). Cut into 1/4-inch chunks (you will need about 2 cups).

Put brown sugar, oil, eggs, and vanilla into a large bowl and beat smooth with a wire whisk. Using a wooden spoon, stir in the flour mixture. Stir in the cranberries, apples, and nuts. The batter will be stiff.

Spread the batter in the prepared pan and bake until a wooden pick inserted in the center of the cake comes out clean, about 1 hour and 5 to 15 minutes.

Place the pan on a wire rack to cool for about 30 minutes. Loosen the edges of the cake and invert on the rack. Let cool completely. It is good fresh; or wrap airtight and store overnight at room temperature before serving or freezing.

SWEET MARSALA-ROSEMARY
CORN MEAL CAKE

MAKES **8** TO **10** PORTIONS.

This crumbly cake is great with espresso, cappuccino, or a good, strong French-roast coffee. If you've never tried rosemary or corn meal in a cake before, you're in for a pleasant surprise.

½	*cup golden raisins*
½	*teaspoon dried rosemary leaves, crumbled*
¼	*cup sweet Marsala or Madeira wine*
½	*cup whole unblanched almonds*
1	*cup all-purpose flour*
1	*cup yellow or white corn meal*
⅔	*cup granulated sugar*
8	*tablespoons unsalted butter*
1	*large egg*
1	*tablespoon confectioners' sugar, or an additional tablespoon granulated sugar*

8-INCH ROUND CAKE PAN OR 8-INCH SPRINGFORM PAN

Soak the raisins and rosemary in the wine for 1 hour at room temperature or, covered, up to 24 hours. (Or microwave 4 minutes on high, until the raisins are plump; cool before using.)

Heat the oven to 350°F. If using a cake pan, line it with

foil, letting the foil extend over the edge a little so you can lift the cake out.

Grind the almonds as fine as possible in a food processor, or in two batches in a blender. Pour into a bowl. Add the flour, corn meal, and the ⅔ cup sugar. Stir to mix well.

Add the butter and cut in with a pastry blender and/or rub in with your fingers, until the mixture is in coarse crumbs. Add the egg to the Marsala-raisin mixture, and beat with a fork to break up the egg. Add to the flour mixture. Stir with the fork until moistened and well blended. The mixture will hold together in small clumps. Press it evenly in the pan and sprinkle with confectioners' or granulated sugar.

Bake about 35 minutes, until the cake is a deep golden brown and a wooden pick inserted in the center comes out clean, about 35 to 40 minutes. (Color is the main clue here; the pick may come out clean before the cake is cooked enough.) Place the pan on a wire rack to cool for 10 minutes then lift out the cake by the foil (or loosen and remove the sides of the springform pan) and place it on the rack. Cool at least 30 minutes before serving. Or cool completely, wrap airtight, and store up to 1 week at room temperature.

Food processor method: Soak the raisins and rosemary. Grind the almonds in the food processor. Add the flour, corn meal, and sugar. Process briefly to blend. Cut up and add the butter; process just until the mixture is in very small pieces. Add the egg; process briefly to blend. The mixture will come together in a clump. Turn it onto a work surface. Knead in the raisins and any remaining wine. Press into the pan. Sprinkle with sugar and bake as directed.

CHOCOLATE-ORANGE CRUMB CAKE

MAKES **12** TO **14** PORTIONS.

Serve this luxurious cake midafternoon or as a dessert. It is very moist, almost wet, so have forks handy.

2	cups all-purpose flour
1½	teaspoons baking powder
½	teaspoon baking soda
¼	teaspoon salt
8	tablespoons unsalted butter
¾	cup granulated sugar
1	cup plain yogurt or buttermilk
2	large eggs
1	teaspoon freshly grated orange peel
½	teaspoon vanilla extract

CRUMB MIXTURE

½	cup granulated sugar
¼	cup unsweetened cocoa powder
3	tablespoons unsalted butter, cut in small pieces
2	teaspoons freshly grated orange peel

9 × 5 × 3-INCH LOAF PAN

Heat the oven to 350°F. Grease the pan.

Put the flour, baking powder, baking soda, and salt into a large bowl. Stir to mix well.

Melt the butter in a small saucepan over very low heat (or

in a large glass measure in a microwave oven). Remove from the heat and stir in the sugar, yogurt, eggs, orange peel, and vanilla. Whisk or stir until well blended.

Put all the ingredients for the crumb mixture into a small bowl and work with your fingertips until the mixture is blended and in small particles.

To make the cake, pour the egg mixture over the flour mixture and stir with a wooden spoon just until blended.

Spread about half the batter in the prepared pan and sprinkle with half the crumb mixture. Cover with the remaining batter and crumbs. To marbleize the crumbs and batter slightly, hold a table knife upright in the batter at one end of the pan. Zigzag from side to side of the pan six to eight times until you reach the other end.

Bake until a wooden pick inserted in the center of the cake comes out moist, but without any uncooked batter clinging to it, about 1 hour. Place the pan on a wire rack to cool at least 30 minutes. Loosen the edges of the cake. Turn out onto the rack and turn over. Let cool completely. Wrap airtight and keep 1 day at room temperature or freeze.

NEWMARKET CAKE

A favorite in the racing country around Newmarket, England, this handsome cake is a good "keeper." It makes a great tailgate cake. It is also good with afternoon tea, or with coffee and a glass of sherry late in the evening.

3	ounces semisweet chocolate (not chips)
2	tablespoons instant coffee crystals
³/4	cup water
2	teaspoons vanilla extract
8	tablespoons unsalted butter, at room temperature
1¹/4	cups granulated sugar
4	large eggs
1	tablespoon baking powder
¹/4	teaspoon salt
3	cups all-purpose flour
²/3	cups pecans or almonds, chopped coarse

10 × 4-INCH TUBE PAN OR 9-INCH SPRINGFORM

Heat the oven to 325°F. Grease the pan.

Chop the chocolate into approximately ¹/4-inch chunks (some pieces will be this big; many will be smaller). Stir the coffee crystals into the water; add the vanilla.

Beat the butter and sugar in the large bowl of an electric

mixer on high speed 3 to 4 minutes, until pale and fluffy, scraping down the sides two or three times.

Beat in the eggs, one at a time. Beat in the baking powder and salt. With the mixer on low, add about one-third of the flour, then, without waiting for it to be completely mixed in, add about one-third of the coffee mixture. Continue until all the flour and coffee mixture has been added, mixing only until blended. Mix in the chocolate and nuts.

Spread the batter in the prepared pan. Bake until the cake is springy to the touch and a wooden pick inserted in the center of the cake comes out clean, 55 to 65 minutes.

Place the pan on a wire rack to cool for about 1 hour. Loosen the edges of the cake with a knife, turn out onto the rack, and turn over. Let cool completely. Serve fresh or wrap airtight and store overnight at room temperature or freeze.

ARMAGNAC, PRUNE, AND WALNUT TEA BREAD

MAKES **12** TO **14** PORTIONS.

Wonderfully boozy. Just right with a cup of tea or coffee, or even a small glass of the same Armagnac you put in the cake. Plan ahead because the prunes need to soak at least 12 hours before you make the cake.

1	cup (7 ounces) pitted prunes
1/2	cup Armagnac or Cognac or brandy (for milder flavor, use 1/3 cup spirits plus 2 tablespoons water)
8	tablespoons unsalted butter, at room temperature
1/2	cup packed light brown sugar
2	large eggs
1	teaspoon vanilla extract
1	teaspoon baking powder
1/4	teaspoon baking soda
1/4	teaspoon salt
1	cup whole-wheat flour
1	cup walnuts, chopped coarse

9 × 5 × 3-INCH LOAF PAN

Oil a knife or kitchen scissors and snip or cut each prune into 10 or 12 pieces (very small prunes into 6 or 8). Place in a bowl with the Armagnac, cover, and let stand at room temperature for at least 12 hours—or up to a week in the refrigerator.

Heat the oven to 350°F. Grease the pan.

In a large bowl beat the butter and sugar with an electric mixer on high speed 3 or 4 minutes, until pale and fluffy. Beat in the eggs, one at a time, scrape down the sides of the bowl. Beat in the vanilla, baking powder, baking soda, and salt. Scrape the bowl.

With the mixer on low speed, beat in the flour until almost blended. Mix in the prunes (including any remaining liquid) and walnuts, just until blended.

Spread the batter in the prepared pan. Bake until a wooden pick inserted in the center of the cake comes out clean, 35 to 40 minutes.

Place the pan on a wire rack to cool 20 to 25 minutes. Loosen the edges of the bread with a knife, turn out onto the rack, and turn over. Let cool completely. Serve fresh, or wrap airtight and store at room temperature for up to 3 days. Freeze for longer storage.

BRANDIED CURRANT TEA BREAD

MAKES **12** TO **14** PORTIONS.

G reat with afternoon tea but even better late at night with espresso and Cognac. Try taking a loaf on your next tailgate picnic. This is what a fruitcake should taste like but never does.

1	cup Zante currants
1/2	cup Cognac or good brandy
10	tablespoons unsalted butter, at room temperature
1	cup granulated sugar
3	large eggs
1	teaspoon baking powder
1	teaspoon vanilla extract
1/4	teaspoon salt
2	cups all-purpose flour
1	cup toasted fine-chopped almonds

9 × 5 × 3-INCH LOAF PAN

Soak the currants in Cognac for at least 1 hour at room temperature—or, covered, in the refrigerator for up to 3 weeks.

Heat the oven to 325°F. Grease the pan.

Electric mixer method (food processor method follows): Put the butter and sugar in a large bowl and beat with an electric mixer on high speed 3 to 5 minutes, until pale and fluffy. Add the eggs, one at a time, beating after each.

With the mixer on low, add baking powder, vanilla, and salt. When ingredients are well mixed, scrape down the sides of the bowl. Add about one-third of the flour, and without waiting for it to be completely mixed in, add the remaining flour in the same way. Scrape the bowl. Add almonds and soaked currants (including any remaining Cognac); mix just until blended.

Pour the batter into the prepared pan. Bake until the cake is lightly browned and springy to the touch about 1 hour and 15 minutes. A wooden pick inserted in the center should come out almost clean but with no uncooked batter sticking to it. Place the pan on a wire rack to cool for 30 to 40 minutes. Loosen the edges of the cake with a knife. Turn it out and turn over. Let cool completely. Serve freshly made, or wrap airtight and store up to 5 days at room temperature, or freeze.

Food processor method: Soak the currants as directed. No need to chop the nuts. Put the butter, sugar, and vanilla in a food processor; process about 1 minute, until pale and fluffy. Break in the eggs, one at a time. Scrape the sides of the bowl. Add the baking powder and salt. Process briefly to blend. Add the flour and nuts. Process a few seconds to blend in the flour and chop the nuts fine. Add the currants and any remaining Cognac. Process, using on/off motion, 2 or 3 times to mix in the currants without chopping them. Bake as directed above.

SUNFLOWER-SEED BROWN-RICE TEA BREAD

MAKES **12** PORTIONS.

Friends on a gluten-free diet will especially appreciate the rich flavor of this crunchy-with-sunflower-seeds tea bread. Brown-rice flour (which, unlike wheat flour, is gluten free) gives a crumbly texture. Be sure the brown-rice flour is fresh and not rancid. The store should have it under refrigeration. This bread is also delicious served warm and freshly baked for breakfast or with morning coffee.

2½ *cups (12 ounces) brown-rice flour*
½ *cup (3 ounces) hulled, but not toasted, sunflower seeds*
¾ *cup packed light brown sugar*
1 *teaspoon baking powder*
½ *teaspoon baking soda*
½ *teaspoon salt*
2 *large eggs, or the equivalent in cholesterol-free egg product*
½ *cup light olive or vegetable oil*
¼ *cup water*

8½ × 4½ × 2¾-INCH LOAF PAN

Heat the oven to 350°F. Grease the pan (be careful not to use one of the cooking sprays that contain flour).

Food processor method (hand method follows): Put the rice flour, sunflower seeds, brown sugar, baking powder, baking soda, and salt into a food processor. Process about 1 minute to chop the seeds fine.

Add the eggs or egg product, the oil, and the water. Process a few seconds to blend well.

Pour the batter into the prepared pan and bake until a wooden pick inserted in the center of the cake comes out clean, 60 to 65 minutes. Place the pan on a wire rack to cool for 20 to 30 minutes. Loosen the edges of the cake with a knife. Turn it out of the pan and turn over. Serve warm. Or cool completely and wrap airtight before storing up to 4 days at room temperature, or freezing.

Hand method: Grind the seeds in an electric blender. Put into a large bowl. Add the flour, sugar, baking powder, baking soda, and salt. Stir to mix well. Add the eggs, oil, and water. Stir and beat to blend well. Bake as directed above.

BROWN-RICE AND NUT TEA BREAD

Follow the directions for Sunflower-Seed Brown-Rice Tea Bread but use ½ cup toasted almonds, pecans, or hazelnuts instead of the sunflower seeds.

KUCHENS

BLUEBERRY-RASPBERRY KUCHEN

Serve warm for dessert with vanilla yogurt or with sour cream lightly sweetened and flavored with vanilla. Any leftovers taste good cold, too.

SOFT COOKIE CRUST

1½	cups all-purpose flour
⅓	cup granulated sugar
¾	teaspoon baking powder
7	tablespoons unsalted butter
1	large egg

FILLING

4	cups (1½ pints) fresh blueberries
1	tablespoon all-purpose flour
⅓	cup seedless red raspberry preserves (damson plum is good too)

9- TO 9½-INCH SPRINGFORM PAN

Heat the oven to 350°F.

Food processor method for crust (hand method follows): Put flour, sugar, and baking powder into a food processor. Process 1 second to mix. Cut up and add the butter; process 3 or 4 seconds, until the mixture is crumbly. Scrape the sides and bottom of the bowl. Break the egg over the mixture. Turn the machine on/off a few times, until a soft dough forms.

Spread and/or pat the dough evenly over the bottom and about 1½ inches up the sides of the ungreased pan. Refrigerate while you prepare the filling.

Pick over the blueberries, discarding any stems, leaves, or squashed berries. Rinse and drain the berries; dry on paper towels.

Mix the flour and preserves in a medium-size bowl. Fold in the berries. Spread evenly in the crust. Bake 55 to 60 minutes, or until the crust is lightly browned. Remove from the oven and place the pan on a wire rack. Loosen the edges of the kuchen with a knife and remove the sides of the pan. Let the kuchen cool at least 1 hour before serving. To store, cover loosely and refrigerate up to 1 day. Does not freeze well.

Hand method for crust: Put flour, sugar, and baking powder into a medium-size bowl. Stir to mix well. Cut up and add the butter. Cut in with a pastry blender and/or rub in with your fingers, until the mixture is in coarse crumbs. Add the egg. Stir with a fork or spoon until a smooth, well-blended dough forms.

PLUM-WALNUT KUCHEN

$\mathbf{M}$ake this with any black plums, or with ripe Italian prune plums when they are in season. Expect juice to flow when you cut this kuchen.

SOFT COOKIE CRUST

1½	cups all-purpose flour
½	cup walnuts
⅓	cup granulated sugar
¾	teaspoon baking powder
7	tablespoons unsalted butter
1	large egg

FILLING

½ cup damson-plum jam or other flavorful plum or black-currant jam

About 1¼ pounds ripe black plums (such as Black Beauty, Black Amber, or Friar)

9- TO 9½-INCH SPRINGFORM PAN

Heat the oven to 350°F.

Food processor method for crust (hand method follows): Put the flour, walnuts, sugar, and baking powder into a food processor. Turn the machine on/off a few times until the walnuts are chopped fine. Cut up and add the butter. Process 3 or 4 seconds, until the mixture is crumbly. Scrape the sides and bottom of the bowl. Break the egg over the mixture.

Turn the machine on/off a few times, until a soft dough forms.

Spread and/or pat the dough evenly over the bottom and about 1½ inches up the sides of the ungreased pan. Refrigerate while you prepare the filling.

Stir the preserves in a medium-size bowl. Rinse and dry the plums. Cut each plum into 6 or 8 slices, discarding the pits. Add to the preserves and stir gently to coat.

Spread the plum filling evenly in the crust. Bake until the crust is medium brown, about 45 to 50 minutes.

Place the pan on a wire rack to cool for 10 to 15 minutes. Loosen the edges of the kuchen with a knife and remove the sides of the pan. Let cool at least 1 hour before serving. To store, cover loosely and leave at room temperature or refrigerate up to 1 day. Does not freeze well.

Hand method for crust: Chop the walnuts fine in an electric blender or with a knife. Mix the flour, sugar, and baking powder in a large bowl. Cut up and add the butter. Cut in with a pastry blender and/or rub in with your fingers, until the mixture is in coarse crumbs. Add the nuts and toss to mix. Add the egg. Stir with a fork or spoon until a well-blended dough forms.

SWEDISH APPLE-ALMOND KUCHEN

MAKES 10 PORTIONS.

The soft cookie crust is filled with fresh fruit and an almond mixture.

Soft Cookie Crust

1½	cups all-purpose flour
⅓	cup granulated sugar
¾	teaspoon baking powder
⅛	teaspoon (or slightly less) ground cardamom, or ½ teaspoon vanilla extract
7	tablespoons unsalted butter
1	large egg

Almond Filling

½	cup blanched or unblanched almonds (whole, chopped, or slivered)
½	cup granulated sugar
3	tablespoons all-purpose flour
1	large egg
2	tablespoons unsalted butter
⅛	teaspoon (or slightly less) ground cardamom, or ½ teaspoon vanilla extract
3	medium-size or 4 small Golden Delicious or other aromatic apples Confectioners' sugar

9- TO 9½-INCH SPRINGFORM PAN

Heat the oven to 350°F.

Food processor method for crust (hand method follows): Put flour, sugar, baking powder, and cardamom (if using) into a food processor; process 1 second to mix. Cut up and add the butter. Process 3 or 4 seconds, until the mixture is crumbly. Scrape the sides and bottom of the bowl. Break the egg over the mixture; sprinkle with vanilla (if using). Turn the machine on/off a few times until a soft dough forms.

Spread and/or pat the dough evenly over the bottom and about 1½ inches up the sides of the ungreased pan. Refrigerate while you prepare the filling.

To make the filling: Put almonds, sugar, and flour in a blender or food processor. Process about 1 minute, until almonds are ground fine. Add the egg, butter, and cardamom or vanilla; process until well blended (the mixture will not be absolutely smooth).

Peel, quarter, and core the apples. One at a time, hold each quarter on a cutting board with a cut side down. Using a small, sharp knife, slice each quarter thin, working from stem to blossom end, but not cutting quite all the way through to where the core was. (Each quarter will be sliced, but the slices won't come apart.)

Pour the almond mixture into the cookie crust. Arrange apple quarters side by side, slightly overlapping, in the almond mixture, core sides down. Bake 60 to 65 minutes, until the crust is very golden and the apples are beginning to brown. Place the pan on a wire rack. Loosen the edges of the kuchen with a knife and remove the sides of the pan. Let

continued

cool at least 1 hour. Sprinkle with confectioners' sugar before serving. Or cool completely, cover, and refrigerate. This kuchen keeps several days but does not freeze well.

Hand method for crust: Put flour, sugar, baking powder, and cardamom (if using) into a medium-size bowl. Stir to mix well. Cut up and add the butter. Cut in with a pastry blender and/or rub in with your fingers, until the mixture is in coarse crumbs. Add the egg and vanilla (if using). Stir with a fork or spoon until a smooth, well-blended dough forms.

PEAR-ALMOND KUCHEN

Follow the directions for Swedish Apple-Almond Kuchen but omit the cardamom. Peel, quarter, and core 2 medium-size firm, ripe Bartlett pears. Cut into ½-inch chunks (you need 2 cups). Put into the cookie crust and pour Almond Filling over the top. Bake as directed.

SOUR CHERRY–ALMOND KUCHEN

Follow the recipe for Swedish Apple-Almond Kuchen but omit cardamom and vanilla. Instead, add ¼ teaspoon almond extract to both crust and filling. Pit enough sour cherries (about 12 ounces) to make 2 cups. Or thoroughly drain a 12- or 16-ounce can or jar of pitted sour cherries. Put the cherries in the crust and pour Almond Filling over them. Bake as directed.

VANILLA PEAR CUSTARD KUCHEN

Be sure to use ripe, aromatic pears. Bartletts work well.

SOFT COOKIE CRUST

1½ cups all-purpose flour
⅓ cup granulated sugar
¾ teaspoon baking powder
7 tablespoons unsalted butter
1 large egg
½ teaspoon vanilla extract

FILLING

3 ripe Bartlett pears (about 6 ounces each)
½ cup reduced-fat or regular sour cream
1 large egg
¼ cup granulated sugar
1 tablespoon all-purpose flour
1 teaspoon vanilla extract

9- TO 9½-INCH SPRINGFORM PAN

Heat the oven to 350°F.

Food processor method for crust (hand method follows): Put the flour, sugar, and baking powder into a food processor. Process 1 second to mix. Cut up and add the butter. Process 3 or 4 seconds, until the mixture is crumbly. Scrape the

continued

sides and bottom of the bowl. Break the egg over the mixture. Sprinkle with vanilla. Turn the machine on/off a few times until a soft dough forms.

Spread or pat the dough evenly over the bottom and 1 to 1½ inches up the sides of the pan.

Peel the pears, quarter lengthwise, and remove the cores. Slice the pears thin from stem end to blossom end. Scatter the fruit over the crust. Bake 30 minutes.

Measure the sour cream in a 2-cup or larger measure. Add the remaining ingredients and whisk to blend. Drizzle over the fruit. Shake the pan gently to settle the custard. Bake 18 to 20 minutes longer, until the custard is no longer liquid in the center (it should be creamy). Place the pan on a wire rack to cool for 5 minutes. Loosen the edges of the kuchen with a knife and remove the sides of the pan. Let cool completely before serving. Refrigerate after 1 hour. Leftovers are very good cold.

Hand method for crust: Put flour, sugar, and baking powder into a medium-size bowl. Stir to mix well. Cut up and add the butter. Cut in with a pastry blender and/or rub in with your fingers, until the mixture is in coarse crumbs. Add the egg and vanilla. Stir with a fork or spoon until a smooth, well-blended dough forms.

VANILLA APPLE CUSTARD KUCHEN

Follow directions for Vanilla Pear Custard Kuchen but use 3 medium-size Golden Delicious or other aromatic apples instead of the pears. Bake as directed.

LEMONY APPLE KUCHEN

The flavor is delicious but the kuchen looks rather plain, so sift a little confectioners' sugar over the top just before serving.

SOFT COOKIE CRUST
1½   cups all-purpose flour
⅓   cup granulated sugar
¾   teaspoon baking powder
7   tablespoons unsalted butter
1   large egg

FILLING
1   large egg
¼   cup granulated sugar
1   tablespoon all-purpose flour
1   teaspoon freshly grated lemon peel
1¼ to 1½ pounds Granny Smith or other tart apples

9- TO 9½-INCH SPRINGFORM PAN

Food processor method for crust (hand method follows): Put flour, sugar, and baking powder into a food processor. Process 1 second to mix. Cut up and add the butter; process 3 or 4 seconds, until the mixture is crumbly. Scrape the sides and bottom of the bowl. Break the egg over the mixture. Process a few seconds, until a soft dough forms.

continued

Spread and/or pat the dough evenly over the bottom and about 1½ inches up the sides of the ungreased pan. Refrigerate while you prepare the filling. Heat the oven to 350°F.

Put the egg, sugar, flour, and lemon peel into a medium-size bowl. Whisk to blend well.

Wash the apples. Shred them either in a food processor or on the coarse side of a grater, shredding them down to the core (no need to peel or cut up the apples first). As each apple is shredded, add the shreds to the egg mixture and stir to coat.

Spread the filling evenly in the kuchen crust. Bake until the crust is medium brown around the edges, about 45 minutes. Place the pan on a wire rack. Loosen the edges of the kuchen with a knife and remove the sides of the pan. Let cool at least 2 hours before serving. To store, cover and refrigerate up to 2 days. Does not freeze well.

Hand method for crust: Put the flour, sugar, and baking powder into a medium-size bowl. Stir to mix well. Cut up and add the butter. Cut in with a pastry blender and/or rub in with your fingers, until the mixture is in coarse crumbs. Add the egg. Stir with a fork or spoon until a smooth, well-blended dough forms.

HARVEST TART

MAKES **8** PORTIONS.

A divine combination of nuts and dried fruits, this kuchen makes a perfect dessert or coffeecake any time during the fall or winter holiday season. Try it for Thanksgiving. The flavor is even better the next day, so you can easily make this ahead. Instead of using already-mixed dried fruits, you can mix your own, using dried apples, apricots, prunes, and, if you wish, pears and raisins. Prepare the filling while the nuts toast.

SOFT COOKIE CRUST

1	cup hazelnuts
1/2	cup granulated sugar
1 1/2	cups all-purpose flour
3/4	teaspoon baking powder
7	tablespoons unsalted butter
1	large egg

FILLING

1 1/2	cups water
	One 11-ounce package mixed dried fruits (almost 3 cups), or your own combination
2	tablespoons lemon juice
1	tablespoon brandy

continued

TOPPING
2 *tablespoons unsalted butter*
2 *tablespoons all-purpose flour*

9- TO 9½-INCH SPRINGFORM PAN

Heat the oven to 350°F. Spread the hazelnuts in a baking pan and bake 10 to 15 minutes, shaking the pan once or twice, until the nuts smell toasty and turn light brown.

Wrap the nuts in a dish towel and rub to loosen the skins. Pick out the nuts; some skins will adhere—not to worry.

Food processor method for crust (blender method follows): Process the nuts and the sugar until the nuts are ground fine. Remove ½ cup of the mixture and save for the topping.

Add the flour and baking powder to the work bowl. Process a few seconds to mix. Cut up and add the butter. Process 3 or 4 seconds until the mixture is crumbly. Scrape the sides and bottom of the bowl. Break the egg over the mixture. Turn the machine on/off a few times until a soft dough forms.

Spread and/or pat the dough evenly over the bottom and about 1½ inches up the sides of the ungreased pan. Fill right away or refrigerate.

To make the filling: Bring the water to a boil in a medium-size saucepan. Snip or cut the fruit into ½-inch pieces. Add it to the water and simmer 8 to 10 minutes, until most of the liquid has been absorbed. Remove from the heat. Stir in lemon juice and brandy. Let cool 10 minutes.

To make the topping: Put the reserved ½ cup nuts and sugar back into the food processor. Add the butter and flour. Process 1 or 2 seconds, until crumbly.

Spread the warm filling in the crust. Sprinkle with the topping. Bake about 40 minutes, until the crust is medium brown. Place the pan on a wire rack to cool for 15 to 20 minutes. Loosen the edges of the kuchen with a knife and remove the sides of the pan. Serve the tart warm. Or cool completely, cover loosely, and store overnight at room temperature.

By hand and electric blender: Grind the toasted hazelnuts in the blender in one or two batches. Put them into a large bowl. Add the sugar and mix well. Remove ½ cup of the mixture and reserve for the topping. To the nuts and sugar remaining in the bowl, add the 1½ cups flour and the baking powder. Stir to mix well. Cut up and add the butter. Cut in with a pastry blender and/or rub in with your fingers, until the mixture is in coarse crumbs. Add the egg. Stir with a fork or wooden spoon until a firm dough forms. Line the pan with the dough and prepare the filling as above. Put the reserved ½ cup sugar and nuts into a small bowl. Add the butter and flour for the topping. Work with your fingers or a fork until well blended and crumbly. Sprinkle the topping over the fruit and bake as directed above.

PEACHES-AND-CREAM KUCHEN

Very easy to make and great to take to a meeting or morning coffee gathering. It's also very good made with fresh nectarines. However, in winter and any time you can't buy really good, ripe fresh peaches (not woolly-textured ones), use canned peaches. You can count on them to be consistent.

SOFT COOKIE CRUST
- 2 cups all-purpose flour
- 1/2 cup granulated sugar
- 1 teaspoon baking powder
- 10 tablespoons unsalted butter
- 2 large eggs
- 2 teaspoons vanilla extract

FILLING AND TOPPING
- 2 pounds ripe peaches or nectarines (6 medium-sized); or one 29-ounce can and one 16-ounce can sliced peaches packed in light syrup, fruit juice, or heavy syrup, thoroughly drained
- 1 cup reduced-fat or regular sour cream
- 2 large eggs
- 1/3 cup granulated sugar (reduce to 1/4 cup if using canned peaches)

2   tablespoons all-purpose flour
1   tablespoon vanilla extract

13 × 9 × 2-INCH BAKING PAN OR DISH

Heat the oven to 350°F.

Food processor method for crust (hand method follows): Put flour, sugar, and baking powder into a food processor. Process 1 to 2 seconds to mix. Cut up and add the butter. Process a few seconds, until the mixture is crumbly. Scrape the bottom and sides of the bowl. Break the eggs over the mixture. Sprinkle with vanilla. Process a few seconds longer, until a soft dough forms.

Spread and pat the dough evenly over the bottom of the ungreased pan. (Dampen or lightly flour your hands if the dough is very sticky.) Refrigerate while you prepare the fruit.

If using fresh peaches, dip 2 or 3 at a time into a saucepan of boiling water; leave 15 to 20 seconds, then remove with a slotted spoon and rinse in cold water to stop them from cooking. Pull off the peel. Cut each peach or nectarine (no need to peel nectarines) into 10 to 12 wedges. Arrange in 4 or 5 crosswise rows on top of the dough (5 will be a tight fit). If using canned peaches, drain thoroughly on paper towels before arranging on the dough.

Bake 30 minutes. Meanwhile, measure sour cream in a 2-cup or larger measure. Add the remaining filling ingredients and whisk to blend well.

Drizzle the custard over the peaches. It won't seem like

continued

enough but don't worry. Shake the pan back and forth gently until the custard is in an even layer. Bake 20 to 22 minutes longer, until the custard is set in the middle (it will firm more on cooling). Place the pan on a wire rack to cool. Do not leave the kuchen at room temperature for more than 1 hour; cover and refrigerate up to 3 days. Let come to room temperature before serving. Do not freeze. Cut into squares and serve from the pan.

Hand method for crust: Mix flour, sugar, and baking powder in a medium-size bowl. Cut up and add the butter. Cut in with pastry blender and/or rub in with your fingers, until the mixture is in coarse crumbs. Add the eggs and vanilla. Stir with a fork until a smooth, well-blended dough forms.

INDEX